FLIGHT

S. E. McKenzie

DEDICATION
To everyone who has been left out in the cold

THIS BOOK IS A BOOK OF SPECULATIVE FICTION
Characters, companies, governments, places, events, are either products of the author's imagination or used fictitiously. Any resemblance to persons (living or dead), companies, governments, places and/or events, is a coincidence and unintentional.

TABLE OF CONTENTS

FLIGHT

I

Breaking sound barrier; what a show
Money burning
In the air

Prestige
On display
Praise to the War Machine

That you don't see every day.
Some machines spy
Others fly; breaking the speed of sound.

Pointy nose;
Heavy; aiming for the ground
Trigger Words; Fibber Words

Super Sonic Boom;
Shock Waves left behind
As Beautiful War Machine breaks the speed of sound;

We heard thunder as we stood on the ground;
A cold shiver made us tremble in fear.
"Fear feeds paranoia and takes control."

A ghost called Joe said to a ghost called Bill.

"Our Beautiful War Machine does more than just kill
It gives everyone
A thrill,"

Joe Replied, wishing that he had not died.

"The War Machine's role is to keep us in control;
When we were human we had nothing
But praise for the cosmic disturbance."

Bill the ghost sighed as he knocked on Heaven's Door.

Heaven; a Place
Humans cannot know
For it is said; they have never been there before.

II
Only lack of fuel can slow
The Beautiful War Machine
As it breaks the sound barrier

FLIGHT

Flying Inquisitor
Searching out for
The Unwanted Visitor.

Flying Inquisitor
Takes flight and hurries out of sight;
Shiny dot in the sky

Shrinking the vastness of our Airspace
Designed to fit
The Flying Inquisitor's orders

Urgency to find the spot
And to drop
Payload after the Cosmic Boom.

Feels like thunder on the ground
This is not the sound of Secret Love
Penetrating into the sky above

This is a world turned upside down
Where the Glass Ceiling
Becomes the floor

And we try to hold on to what we had before.

When Secret Love grew unconditionally
When wealth was divided
And multiplied freely

Frozen moment in time
Secret Love which kept hope alive
Refusing to be alienated nor baited.

Hoping to find the secret
We are not meant
To know

For that secret door
Was said to be forbidden
To humans; for evermore

As the Flying Inquisitor
Turned our world upside down
The Glass Ceiling became the floor

While we held on to what we had before.

FLIGHT

A world; not ours to know any more.
We are the prey
Of the Flying Inquisitor

We wait for our darkest hour
Hoping that the secret door
Will be open to us that day.

It is said that the secret door
Is not yours nor mine
Nor owned by the Flying Inquisitor

Still the Flying Inquisitor
Can turn the world
Upside down

Where the Glass Ceiling
Becomes the floor
And we try to hold on to what we had before

As we try
To find the key;
To the secret door

Lies in one's Soul-head
Bill the Ghost said to Joe the ghost
Remembering how the steel nose

Pulled him down too fast;

We all hear each other's fear
After the Sonic Boom
Brings some joy; other's gloom.

Moisture in the air; forming into water droplets
Clouds grow;
Nature's Way;

The Supersonic Eye
Sees all; heavy nose knows;
Justice is blind

Not easily defined
Behind the curtain of protocol;
Amidst the thunder; Nature's call;

King of Vitriol
Blamed us all
When the cake could not rise

FLIGHT

He told us we could eat the flat cake
Anyway
And then wished us a good day

The Flying Inquisitor
Targets
Dehumanized prey

Harming those that get in between;
The scene is mean
But the Flying Inquisitor

Cannot be seen
By men with less
Than Men of Fortune

Angry tone
Targeting those all alone
Men of Fortune; cold as stone

Turning our world upside down
Glass Ceiling becomes the floor
While we hang on to what we had before.

Men of Fortune
Fondle their weapons of choice
To lord over the Broken Hearted;

Men of Fortune
So brave behind their Beautiful War Machines
They only share Secret Love when they whisper

Coward; they target those alone
Can't be called a crime
For their self-appointed authority

Lifts them above it all
So they can watch
Those beneath crawl

In the upside down world
Where the Glass Ceiling
Becomes the floor

Not much left
They have it all
Men of Fortune; Men of History;

FLIGHT

Men fondling their weapons while causing misery
Too numb;
The weary people bow their heads.

While Men of Fortune
Roam inside places
Blown off the map

Steely gate
Without a key
Surrounds those who hunger to be free;

Forced to live a life of pain and sorrow
So afraid of Tomorrow;
Men with Machine Nose in the air

Too heavy; Gravity pulls Machine Nose down to Earth.

Now pointing to the ground;
Machine Nose points up into the air;
Again.

Travels faster than sound;
Thunder cracks by our feet on the ground;
Lost time; condensed space;

Just another face
Ageing behind a frown
Anger once the tool now the foe;

Creating a scene
Hoping the foe will lose control
And then they will fly away

Into their world
That they own everyday
While hanging on

The fool forgets about tomorrow
Shock waves
Created as steel nose

Grows too heavy
And must come down
For it takes a lot of fuel

To travel against gravity
Just another Force at work
Treating those below

FLIGHT

As if they were a jerk.
Must know your own mind;
Beyond skin;

Never letting outside in.

Callous Man
Sees too much misery
Can no longer be kind;

Why would he let outside in?
Pride which arrogates the willfully blind;
Above our heads; so high we cannot see;

I hear the sonic roar
Breaking the sound barrier; can't be ignored
Even though it can't be seen

The pride which it is arrogating
Is mean, overseen by no one;
Spinning around in the air

The mighty feeling
Faster than sound
Sometimes breaks the windows on the ground.

Freedom to arrogate power
Too much might
From the air

Brings down steely nose
No balance;
Pulled into Gravity's glance.

"We fly in this immense sky
We see nothing but emptiness
Looming in the Horizon every day

We must fly for it is the only life we know,"
Bill the ghost said to Joe the ghost
"Now if we could only see

What lies on the other side
Of Heaven's Door," Joe replied.
Could be peace we were looking for

Before we died."

And I knew Peace
Was just a promise
Waiting for us; at Heaven's Door.

FLIGHT

Emptiness in the horizon; shrunk
By super-sonic flight
The roaring thunder in the night

Gentle world
Somewhere above
Is said to exist

So easy to miss
We heard a crack on the ground
We knew the meaning of the sound

Sonic Boom had brought gloom
To many who now felt doom
And Might be frozen in hate

Micromanagement; mismanagement;
Disengaged from the pain
Targeted for harsher rules

We dodge Smirking Fools

The enemy described in the script
The enemy that we never meet
The enemy that will never admit defeat.

Enemy competes with the boss
Enemy who contributes to our loss
The enemy is more like us

Than we will ever know.

The enemy of the master mind
Competes for the wealth all around
In the vast world shrunk by sonic flight

Flying in the middle of the night
Showing might
While the master-mind calls this right

The Flying Inquisitor
Looking for the Uninvited Visitor
Who knows Freedom is just in the mind

As he roams into the Negative Zone
He never felt so alone
For the people there have hearts of stone

Micromanaged; mismanaged;
Targets are hidden in System Code;
Sonic Boom; success for some;

For others life grows into gloom and doom.

FLIGHT

Wasteland way too soon.
Emptiness
Inside Out

The Flying Inquisitor
Turning the world upside down
Glass Ceiling becomes the floor

We hang on to everything that we had before.

As the Mass Mind closed
The Mass Mind became smaller
Trapped in tunnel vision

No expected objectivity in their decision.

III
"How can we be civilized?
In such a barbaric world?"
I wondered to myself

As Impulsive Noise
Adjusted to our manufactured consent
Our voice could not be heard; unknown was our Content.

A fact; an assumption or an act
No one knows what is true
Anymore.

No channel of communication
When we needed it the most
Cold air surrounded us

And some said ghosts from a lost time
Were drawing near
Ghosts who wrote rules a long time ago;

To disrupt the flow
Of thought; decay turned to rot
And overruled any discussion

The Inquisitor was paid to win the argument;
"First one through the wall
Will be the first one to fall,"

I heard a ghostly voice complain
I was surrounded by cold air
One more time again.

Unwritten protocol;
The masters' call;
Too sad to walk tall;

FLIGHT

Protocol;
Unwritten policy
Followed before Tea.

A fact; an assumption or an act
No one knows what is true
Anymore.

IV

Vast sky
An ancient world's Ceiling
Lost in the cold; unappealing;

Flight Path;
Wildlife scatters out of the way
Super Sonic Might

A fright
For birds in flight
Looking for worms

Hiding beneath the light
Of day
Nature's way

In the night
A watcher said,
"Watch out for predators dear.

They are near those who walk.
They will pretend to want to talk
And you will be too tired to fight

A hard line that we must repeat
Never admit defeat
Only the chosen few would ever be elite

Fewer could afford to eat
Starvation became hidden
Truth became forbidden

For time is ticking away the day
Weakening Strength; Lost Might;
If caught you will die in fright."

We could hear the Flying Inquisitor
Overhead
Turning our world upside down

FLIGHT

What was once the Glass Ceiling
Was now a floor
As we hung on to everything that we had before.

In the land which could not innovate
Many were controlled in feelings of hate
And could never be free.

It was now the middle of the night
I knew that I must take refuge
And find

A tree that I could hide behind
And stay until the morning light
Could shine

I didn't need the tree to be mine
For the tree I found was free
Basking in the peace of Nature's Equity

The soul of Equity
Divides and multiplies freely;
From the Creation's heart.

Tree was still standing that night
But fell before the morning light
The Flying Inquisitor

Was still in flight.

To anyone that was not their kind
Many became willfully blind
To their cruelty

Which destroyed Equity
While we tried to blend
Into the ground

Without getting buried there
We still had a lot to share
And believed Equity would re-balance

One day soon
Equity would touch this Valley of Doom
If we kept an open mind

The machines took the jobs
And the brown shirts were used to
Blending individuals into mobs

FLIGHT

They were picked for size
Often despised
Pride allowed them to stare

As if I wasn't there
I was too young to have lost my dream
As barriers went up to create a new revenue stream

We are waiting until the debt bubble pops
The brown shirts are wanna be cops
Disengaged and micro-managed;

They did not know what could have been
There was not much that they had ever seen
Chaos was disguised

In Stereotypes and hype
To devalue Content
So Fools could rule.

We knew

The Inquisition was in full swing
The Cosmic Boom
Would made our ears ring

Even though we hoped

The human part of the Inquisitor
Would give us something to salvage
He had grown too savage

And was turning the world upside down
The Glass Ceiling became the floor
While we hung on to all we had before.

The Inquisition
Destruction of Competition
The new Bigotry

Hard to see
Was a state of mind
Made some willfully blind

But the Tree was still standing
Symbol of Equity
Nature's Way

As the darkness of the night
Created invisibility
Only the moon shone nearby;

FLIGHT

While I found myself alone
Waking up underneath
A fallen tree

With bird poop all over me

I had a piece of bread
Which I shared
With the birds that were not dead

They shared a song with me
Which lingered in in my head
Promising a better day

Bringing on a new way
Once the night of horror had faded
Leaving my part of town in a pile of rubble.

The Inquisition's smoke
Blocked the sun
No apology needed; damage could not be undone.

I raised my eyes to the sky; above
All this trouble
And I knew it would take

A lot of love
To turn this Inquisition around
For his toxic state of hate

Was soaking into our ground
With a crack,
We heard the Sonic Boom from the air

And we knew
Many more would be
Frozen in hate

Could only sustain
The Negative Zone's Fate
The Inquisition had blocked out the sun

Wasteland
Emptiness
Inside Out

As the Mass Mind closed
It became smaller
Trapped in tunnel vision

FLIGHT

No objectivity in their decision.

As conditions were left to deteriorate
Decay ate until there was nothing there
No one left to care

And we the people knew
If we didn't find a new way soon
It would be too late.

We did not respond to the brown shirts
While they tried to stir up anger
We kept our eyes on our friends above

For they flew closest to Heaven's door
Which one day would open
For those pure enough

Submerged in Secret Love

We strengthened our selves
Refusing to be warehoused on shelves
We waited for the light to burst into the sky

For the new day
Promised a better way;
Giving us time to find the key

S.E. McKENZIE

To the secret door

Somewhere up above
A place where there still was love
Once freed would fill the sky

And tumble down upon us
Still standing
On this scorch

Wasteland
Emptiness
Inside Out

Hoping with all our might that the secret

Would reveal itself to us
And turn our pain into might
We gazed into the sky again

And we could see what the light could do
Made us cover our eyes; it was day
And the sun was too bright

We felt the light's might
And hoped that there was a force
Watching over us.

FLIGHT

The King of Vitriol's rule had begun
The Negative Zone's Fate
Was in his hands

Earth's Equity
Was growing in Her Tree
Nature's Way

As we continued on
We knew every path was being watched
A supersonic bullet overhead

Left Wasteland
And Emptiness
As we looked from Inside Out.

The note on the wall said
All bags must be left
At the door.

THE END

Produced by S.E. McKenzie Productions
First Print Edition August 2015

Enquiries: 1(778)992-2453
Mailing Address:
S. E. McKenzie Productions
168 B 5th St.
Courtenay, BC
V9N 1J4

Email Address:
messidartha@aol.com

http://www.amazon.com/SarahMcKenzie/e/B00H9RWX48/ref=ntt
_dp_epwbk_0

www.ingramcontent.com/pod-product-compliance
Lightning Source LLC
Chambersburg PA
CBHW060547030426
42337CB00021B/4476